Girls Play Basketball

by Yvonne Johnson

Glenview, Illinois • Boston, Massachusetts • Chandler, Arizona
Upper Saddle River, New Jersey

Characters:

- SENDA ABBOTT
- CLARA BAER
- DR. JAMES NAISMITH

Time:

- 1890s

Setting:

- SENDA's living room

Senda Abbott (1868–1954)

Dr. James Naismith
(1861–1939)

SENDA: I am Senda Abbott. I will tell you about basketball. This is Dr. James Naismith. He invented basketball.

JAMES: Yes, I did! I was a gym teacher. In 1891, I invented a new game for boys. They needed a game to play in the winter. That's how basketball started.

SENDA: Basketball was different back then.

JAMES: Yes. The idea was the same, but some things were different.

SENDA: What things were different?

JAMES: We used peach baskets, not hoops! They were made of wood. They held peaches. I used them for the baskets. They were not open at the bottom. The ball did not fall through.

SENDA: What kind of ball did you use?

JAMES: At first, we used a soccer ball. It did not bounce high.

SENDA: Dr. Naismith, do you know people still love basketball today? Now, people watch basketball games on TV.

JAMES: TV...of course! I did not remember that. We did not have TVs back then.

SENDA: *(laughs)* We did not have many girls playing basketball back then, either.

JAMES: That is true. Did you play basketball, Mrs. Abbott?

Soon girls played basketball too.

SENDA: Yes, I did. I worked at Smith College. I taught gym class. I wanted girls to play basketball.

JAMES: At that time, people thought girls had to be careful. They thought girls would get hurt playing sports.

SENDA: I thought that way too. I made up new basketball rules for girls. Today, people have different ideas about girls' sports.

JAMES: Mrs. Abbott, you did a great thing! You helped start women's basketball.

JAMES: Tell us about the rules for girls.

SENDA: *(holds up a drawing)* I divided the court in three parts. Each team had six to ten players. Players stayed in one part of the court. The girls did not have to run so much.

JAMES: What other changes did you make?

SENDA: Girls could not foul each other. They could not push the ball away from other players. I thought this made the game safer.

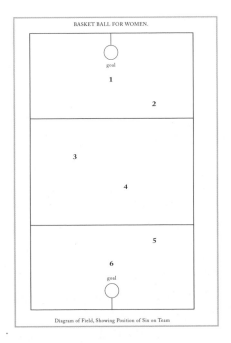

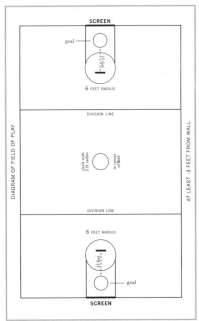

These drawings show how Senda split the court for girls.

CLARA: *(walking in)* I know another change made to basketball for girls.

SENDA: Hello, Clara!

CLARA: I am Clara Gregory Baer. I was a gym teacher too. I am also important in basketball history.

SENDA: Clara heard about basketball. She wanted her girls to play.

CLARA: Some people did not want girls to play. So I made up new rules too.

It was hard for girls to move in long skirts.

CLARA: I called my game "basquette" (bahs KETT). I had many rules. Girls could not talk or yell. I made another big change. Do you remember, Senda?

SENDA: Yes! Your girls were the first to wear bloomers. These were special pants. Before that, girls wore long skirts.

CLARA: That's right! Bloomers made it easier to move. Many girls wore bloomers to play basketball.

It was easier to play wearing special pants, or bloomers.

SENDA: *(to Clara)* Today, girls wear shorts.

JAMES: Do you remember when girls could watch only other girls play basketball? Now, anyone can watch boys and girls.

SENDA: Yes. Today, boys and girls both play basketball. There is only one difference. Girls play with a smaller ball. That's because many girls have smaller hands.

CLARA: *(picking up a basketball and passing it to Senda)*
  I want to play!

SENDA: Why not? Let's play!

JAMES: See you on the basketball court!

ALL: Goodbye, everyone! Have fun playing our game.

BASKETBALL COURT

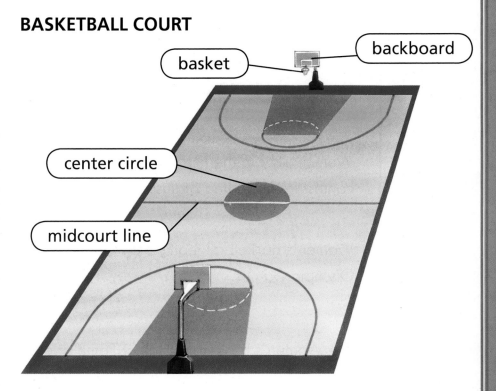

basket

backboard

center circle

midcourt line

Basketball is played by two teams. There are five players on each team. A player shoots the ball through the hoop to score points.

Women's Basketball History

1891	Dr. Naismith invents basketball.
1892	Senda Berenson changes basketball rules for women.
1895	Clara Gregory Baer makes her own rules for women's basketball.
1918	Players use baskets with the bottom open. This was the first "hoop."
1926	Women play in the first big basketball contest in the United States.
1976	Women's basketball teams play in the Olympic Games.
1999	The Women's Basketball Hall of Fame opens.